Children's Authors

Beverly Cleary

Cari Meister
ABDO Publishing Company

visit us at
www.abdopub.com

Published by ABDO Publishing Company, 4940 Viking Drive, Suite 622, Edina, Minnesota 55435. Copyright © 2001 Abdo Consulting Group, Inc., P.O. Box 398166, Minneapolis, Minnesota 55439 USA. International copyrights reserved in all countries. No part of this book may be reproduced in any form without written permission from the publisher.

Printed in the United States.

Photos: Tom McDonough (page 5); Corbis (page 9); Grant High School (page 11); Chaffey Junior College (page 13); University Archives at Bancroft Library, University of California Berkeley - 308s B61938 (page 15); Oregon Historical Society - 001274 (page 17); HarperCollins (page 19); Portland Parks and Recreation (page 21)
Editors: Bob Italia, Tamara L. Britton, Kate A. Furlong, Christine Fournier
Art Direction: Neil Klinepier

Library of Congress Cataloging-in-Publication Data

Meister, Cari.
    Beverly Cleary / Cari Meister.
        p. cm. -- (Children's authors. Set 2)
    Includes bibliographical references and index.
    ISBN 1-57765-480-3
    1. Cleary, Beverly--Juvenile literature. 2. Authors, American--20th century--Biography--Juvenile literature. [1. Cleary, Beverly. 2. Authors, American. 3. Women--Biography.] I. Title. II. Series.

PS3553.L3914 Z785 2001
813'.54--dc21
[B]

00-046929

Contents

Beverly Cleary

*F*or more than 50 years, Beverly Cleary has been writing children's books. Her dream to become a writer began when she was in junior high school. One of Beverly's teachers **complimented** her writing. She encouraged Beverly to become a children's writer.

Beverly liked the idea of becoming a writer. But she also knew she needed a steady job. So in college, she studied to be a librarian. After graduating, she worked as a children's librarian in Washington state.

As Beverly worked, she remembered her dream to write children's books. So in 1949, she sat down to write her first story, *Henry Huggins*. It was published the next year.

Since *Henry Huggins*, Beverly has written more than 40 books. They have won several awards and honors. And they have brought a love of reading to millions of children.

Opposite page: Beverly Cleary

Life in Yamhill

Beverly Atlee Bunn was born in McMinnville, Oregon, on April 12, 1916. She was an only child. Her parents were Lloyd and Mable Bunn.

The Bunns lived on a farm in Yamhill, Oregon. Beverly's father worked the land. Beverly and her mother cooked food, washed laundry, and helped around the farm.

Beverly also had time for fun. She rode on a float in Yamhill's Fourth of July parade. And she was a flower girl on May Day.

Young Beverly loved to hear stories. She had two books of her own, *Mother Goose* and *The Story of the Three Bears*. Her mother often read her these books. She also told Beverly other fairy tales, **fables**, and poems.

Beverly's mother thought Beverly should have some new stories. But Yamhill did not have a library. So Beverly's mom started one. The library grew quickly. Soon, Yamhill children had many new books to choose from.

The Bunns earned little money on the Yamhill farm. So in 1922, they rented out the farm and moved to Portland, Oregon. There, Mr. Bunn hoped to find a job that would pay better.

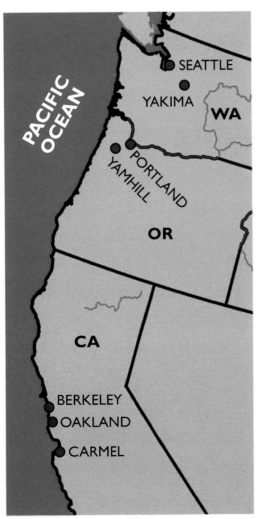

America's West Coast

Throughout her life, Beverly Cleary has made her home in several cities along America's West Coast.

Growing up in Portland

*T*he Bunns rented a house. Mr. Bunn quickly found work as a nighttime security guard. Beverly made friends with children in the neighborhood.

In the fall, Beverly began first grade at Fernwood Grammar School. Her teacher was Mrs. Falb. Mrs. Falb taught the class how to read and do math.

Beverly enjoyed school. Mrs. Falb gave her gold stars for doing good work. But then Beverly caught chicken pox. She missed a week of school. Then Beverly caught **smallpox**. She missed even more school.

Beverly fell behind her classmates. She had an especially hard time with reading. Mrs. Falb put her in the lowest reading group, the Blackbirds. The reading activities made Beverly nervous.

Portland, Oregon

Reader & Writer

*I*n second grade, Beverly had a new teacher named Mrs. Marius. She was kind and patient. She taught Beverly how to read. But Beverly still did not think it was fun.

The next year, Beverly read a book called *The Dutch Twins* by Lucy Fitch Perkins. She liked the story a lot. She realized books could be fun and interesting.

Beverly began to read more often. She wanted to read funny stories about real kids. But she had a hard time finding such stories. Most were about rich children in faraway lands.

At home, money had become tight for the Bunns. So in 1928, they sold the Yamhill farm to make extra money. They used the money to buy a car and a house.

Beverly continued to read and write. In seventh grade, she wrote an **essay** about her favorite book characters. In the essay, a girl visited Bookland. There, she met Beverly's favorite book characters.

The teacher loved Beverly's story. She told the class Beverly should write children's books. Beverly liked the idea. But her mother said she should have a steady job, too. So Beverly decided to become a librarian.

The Great Depression began in 1929. Many people across the country lost their jobs. Mr. Bunn lost his job, too. The Bunns had little money.

In 1930, Beverly began attending Grant High School. She enjoyed school, except for gym class. She and her friends liked to attend dances, watch movies, and listen to radio programs.

Beverly during her senior year at Grant High School

Learning

*B*everly graduated from high school in 1934. Her teachers wanted her to go to college. But the Bunns did not have enough money. Then Beverly received a letter from a relative named Verna Clapp.

Verna lived in California. She invited Beverly to stay with her family. While there, Beverly could attend Chaffey Junior College. It charged no **tuition**. The Bunns agreed to let Beverly go.

Beverly attended Chaffey for two years. She studied hard and made new friends. In 1936, Beverly graduated. But she did not yet have enough training to be a librarian. So she began attending classes at the University of California in Berkeley.

*Beverly's graduation picture
from Chaffey Junior College*

Library Days

At Berkeley, Beverly studied English. While at a dance one night, Beverly met Clarence Cleary. The two soon began dating.

Beverly graduated from Berkeley in 1938. She still wanted to be a librarian. So she attended the School of Librarianship at the University of Washington in Seattle.

At the School of Librarianship, Beverly learned how to **recommend** books, organize a library, and tell interesting stories to children. She graduated in 1939.

Soon, Beverly began working as a librarian. Her first job was at the public library in Yakima, Washington. She worked in the children's room. She helped children find books they would enjoy. And she told them stories during storytime.

While in Yakima, Beverly still dreamed of writing children's books. But her job left little time for writing. Then in 1940, Beverly married Clarence Cleary.

In December 1942, the U.S. entered **World War II**. Beverly took a job as a librarian at an army hospital in Oakland,

California. She talked with wounded soldiers. She learned their interests and ordered books they would enjoy.

Beverly worked at the hospital until **World War II** ended in 1945. Then she and Clarence moved to a house in Berkeley, California. Soon, Beverly began to write the children's book she had dreamed about.

Beverly's 1938 yearbook photo from the University of California, Berkeley

BEVERLY ATLEE BUNN

Portland, Oregon

Letters and Science —English

Transfer from Chaffey Junior College; Masonic Club; Stebbins Hall.

Success as a Writer

*I*n 1949, Beverly wrote her first book. While writing, she tried to remember the kind of books she wanted to read as a child. She had wanted funny stories about real children. So she wrote about a third grade boy and his dog.

Beverly sent her book to the William Morrow and Company **publishing house**. They liked Beverly's book and agreed to publish it. In 1950, *Henry Huggins* was published.

Children loved *Henry Huggins*. They wanted Beverly to write more stories. She continued to create interesting and real characters such as Ellen Tebbits, Otis Spofford, and Beezus Quimby.

Beverly enjoyed writing. But she wanted to have a family, too. In 1955, the Clearys had twins named Malcolm and Marianne. While caring for the twins, Beverly continued to write.

Beverly Cleary poses
for a picture in 1954.

Ramona

*O*ne of Beverly's best-loved characters is Ramona Quimby. She first introduced readers to Ramona in the 1955 book *Beezus and Ramona*. Ramona appeared as Beezus's little sister.

Readers liked the Ramona character. They wanted a book about Ramona. Beverly thought about it for a long time. In 1968, she finally wrote *Ramona the Pest.*

Readers loved learning of Ramona's adventures. So Beverly continued to write Ramona stories. Between 1975 and 1984, she wrote five books about Ramona.

Then Beverly took a break from the Ramona books. But in 1999, she surprised fans by writing a new one. It is called *Ramona's World*.

The Ramona books have earned Beverly fame and awards. *Ramona and Her Father* and *Ramona Quimby, Age 8* were both named **Newbery Honor Books**. And a television series based on the Ramona books aired on PBS in 1988.

Beverly Cleary

Cleary's Fame

Beverly's books have won many awards. In 1975, she won the **Laura Ingalls Wilder Medal**. And in 1984, Beverly's *Dear Mr. Henshaw* won the **Newbery Medal**.

Children across the globe love Beverly's stories. Her books have been **translated** into 14 languages. And her characters have appeared on television shows in the U.S., Canada, Australia, Japan, Spain, Sweden, and Denmark.

Beverly's hometown of Portland, Oregon, honored her in 1995. That year, the city opened the Beverly Cleary Sculpture Garden for Children. It is a park with sculptures of Beverly's characters.

Today, Beverly lives in Carmel, California. Recently, she wrote two **memoirs**. They are called *A Girl from Yamhill* and *On My Own Two Feet*. Beverly also continues to write books for children.

Opposite page: The Ramona statue at the Beverly Cleary Sculpture Garden for Children

Glossary

compliment - something said in praise of a person.

essay - a short, written work on a particular subject.

fable - a story meant to teach a lesson. The characters in fables are usually animals.

Laura Ingalls Wilder Medal - an award given out by the American Library Association to an author or illustrator whose works have made a long-lasting contribution to children's literature.

memoir - a written account of a person's experiences and memories.

Newbery Honor Book - a runner-up to the Newbery Medal award.

Newbery Medal - an award given by the American Library Association to the author of the year's best children's book.

publishing house - a business that produces and offers printed materials for sale to the public.

recommend - to suggest.

smallpox - an illness that causes a fever and rash.

translate - to change from one language to another.

tuition - the money a student pays to receive instruction.

World War II - 1939-1945, fought in Europe, Asia, and Africa. The United States, France, Great Britain, the Soviet Union, and their allies were on one side. Germany, Italy, Japan, and their allies were on the other side. The war began when Germany invaded Poland. America entered the war in 1941 after Japan bombed Pearl Harbor, Hawaii.

Internet Sites

HarperCollins

http://www.harperchildrens.com

Click on MEET THE AUTHOR and then on BEVERLY CLEARY
to find a list of the books Mrs. Cleary has written, awards she
has won, and more!

Write to Mrs. Cleary at:
HarperCollins Children's Books
1350 Avenue of the Americas
New York, NY 10019

*These sites are subject to change. Go to your favorite search engine and
type in Beverly Cleary for more sites.*

Index